Clearing Storm from Bright Angel Lodge. Located on the South Rim, Grand Canyon Village is the center of visitor activity in the Park. While this area shows signs of habitation dating back at least four thousand years, it was first viewed by European eyes about 1540, when Don Garcia Lopez de Cardeñas was brought here by Hopi guides.

FROM THE GRAND CANYON WISH YOU WERE HERE® POSTCARD BOOK

SIERRA PRESS, INC.

PHOTO: © JIM WILSON

Sunrise from Mather Point. The great temples and buttes of the Grand Canyon were formed over many eons, primarily by the force of erosion. Unharnessed run-off from countless storms falling on the Colorado Plateau carved deep gullies and canyons. The joining of these tributaries supplied water volume necessary to create this mile-deep canyon. The varying degree of resistance from each layer accounts for the unique sculpture of each formation.

FROM THE GRAND CANYON WISH YOU WERE HERE® POSTCARD BOOK

SIERRA PRESS, INC.

PHOTO: © DICK DIETRICH

Sunset from Toroweap Overlook. As much as eighteen miles wide and stretching nearly 280 river miles, the Grand Canyon is one of the most spectacular sights on planet Earth. First protected as a National Monument in 1906 by Theodore Roosevelt and made a National Park in 1919 by Woodrow Wilson, the Grand Canyon is additionally protected by international treaty as a World Heritage Site. Visitors from around the world come to gaze in awe and wonder at what President Roosevelt proclaimed to be 'the most impressive piece of scenery I have ever looked at", surely the understatement of the century.

FROM THE GRAND CANYON WISH YOU WERE HERE® POSTCARD BOOK

SIERRA PRESS, INC.

PHOTO: © LARRY ULRICH

Mohave Wall, Winter. Considered by most geologists to be the pre-eminent geologic showcase on earth, the Grand Canyon exposes nearly two-billion years in the history of our planet. The layers of the Canyon tell a remarkable story; of ancient seas; of mountains and deserts; of volcanoes and rivers. For the last several million years the Colorado and its tributaries, in collusion with wind, rain and ice, have been at work here carving 'the most sublime spectacle on earth.'

FROM THE GRAND CANYON WISH YOU WERE HERE® POSTCARD BOOK

SIERRA PRESS, INC.

PHOTO: © JIM WILSON

Claret Cup Cactus. At river level, 5,000 feet below the rim, the environment is typical of Mexico's Sonoran Desert, with blazing summer temperatures relieved occasionally by summer thundershowers. Plants typically found in this region include members of the cacti family, creosote bush, yucca, ocotillo and sage. The riparian zone lining the river, which in places is only a few feet wide, is a rich environment for cottonwood, mesquite, acacia, willow and tamarisk. Few places on Earth provide such a vivid illustration of plant zones.

FROM THE GRAND CANYON WISH YOU WERE HERE® POSTCARD BOOK

SIERRA PRESS, INC.

PHOTO: © GARY LADD

Mt. Hayden From Point Imperial. At an elevation of 8803 feet, Point Imperial is the highest location along the North Rim. It is truly a breathtaking vista of the eastern portion of the Park and the Colorado Plateau beyond. The color and beauty of the Painted Desert sweeps northward leading to views of Navajo Mountain and the pink Vermillion Cliffs. The exposed spire of Mt. Hayden dominates the foreground.

FIRST CLASS POSTAGE REQUIRED

SIERRA PRESS, INC.

PHOTO: © JEFF NICHOLAS

Marble Canyon from below Badger Rapids. "Too thick to drink, too thin to plow" was an early visitor's observation of the Colorado River as it flows through the inner canyon. The Grand Canyon we see today was carved by the mighty forces of erosion in a blink of geologic time, 30 million years. From river level cliffs and buttes form the dominate features of the horizon, often towering thousands of feet above.

FROM THE GRAND CANYON WISH YOU WERE HERE® POSTCARD BOOK

SIERRA PRESS, INC.

PHOTO: © LARRY ULRICH

Matkatamiba Canyon. The oasis of Matkatamiba Canyon offers a delightful respite from the hot, dry environment typical of the Plateau community. As with all water courses in the southwest, it is host to a lush riparian habitat that features flora and fauna quite different from that of its arid surroundings. These plants and animals are virtual prisoners, not able to venture far from their life-giving water.

FROM THE GRAND CANYON WISH YOU WERE HERE® POSTCARD BOOK

SIERRA PRESS, INC.

PHOTO: © LARRY ULRICH

Sunset from Hopi Point. At an elevation of 7000 feet, the South Rim is situated in what is known by geologists as the Canadian zone. This zone features coniferous trees and moderate temperatures. At river level, 5000 feet below, the environment is typical of Mexico's Sonoran Desert, with little rainfall and blazing summer temperatures. Few places on earth provide a glimpse of such varied life zones in one location.

FROM THE GRAND CANYON WISH YOU WERE HERE® POSTCARD BOOK

SIERRA PRESS, INC.

PHOTO: © JEFF NICHOLAS

Aspens, North Rim. At an elevation of 7,000 to 8,800 feet, the rims of the Grand Canyon are situated in, what is known by geologists as, the Canadian zone. This zone is occupied by coniferous forests made up of pine, spruce, hemlock and fir. On the North Rim there are bountiful stands of aspen.

FROM THE GRAND CANYON WISH YOU WERE HERE® POSTCARD BOOK

SIERRA PRESS, INC.

PHOTO: © GARY LADD

Rainbow at Sunset from Yaki Point. In 1857 Lt. Joseph Ives, entering from the west, led a survey party into the Grand Canyon. Ives was not impressed, stating in his report, "Ours has been the first, and will doubtless be the last, party of whites to visit this profitless locality." How wrong he was!, millions will visit each year to look into this 'profitless locality' and view a land beyond description-beyond imagination.

FIRST CLASS POSTAGE REQUIRED

SIERRA PRESS, INC.

PHOTO: © MARK & JENNIFER MILLER

Winter Storm From Sinking Ship Overlook. Several times each year the Canyon is transformed into a Winter wonderland by consecutive heavy snowstorms. Fog obscures the river and shrouds the temples leaving the first time visitor to wonder how deep this canyon really is. Even when snow is extremely heavy on the rim, flakes most often evaporate before reaching the inner canyon.

FROM THE GRAND CANYON WISH YOU WERE HERE® POSTCARD BOOK

SIERRA PRESS, INC.

PHOTO: © JIM WILSON

Sunset, Mather Point. From near Mather Point, Coconino Sandstone reflects the warmth of sunset and shapes of ancient sand dunes. At the brink of the 'Grandest Canyon of all' this prominent overlook is the first view most visitors experience. It was named for Stephen T. Mather, the first director of our National Park Service.

FROM THE GRAND CANYON WISH YOU WERE HERE® POSTCARD BOOK

SIERRA PRESS, INC.

PHOTO: © DICK DIETRICH

Rainbow over Colorado River, Unkar Rapid Area. The Grand Canyon is situated at the apex of the Colorado Plateau. Occupying large areas of Arizona, Utah, Colorado and New Mexico. This region has been carved into a series of canyons by the Green, San Juan, Little Colorado and Escalante Rivers, all converging to form the powerful Colorado River. This region is now host to the largest concentration of National Parks in America.

FROM THE GRAND CANYON WISH YOU WERE HERE® POSTCARD BOOK

FIRST CLASS POSTAGE REQUIRED

SIERRA PRESS, INC.

PHOTO: © TOM TILL